JOURNEY of the YELLOW FEATHER

TANYA TURTON

Copyright © 2020 Tanya Turton

Copyright remains the property of the author and apart from any fair dealing for the purposes of private study,

research, criticism or review, as permitted under the Copyright Act, no part may be reproduced by any process

without written permission. All inquiries should be made to the author.

National Library of Australia - ISBN-9780648873914

I ask only of...

"A LIFE FILLED WITH LOVE"

In my allowing of this to be true.

I look to see of this love every single day.

CHAPTER ONE

I AM THAT I AM

It becomes apparent within oneself this asking that is to arise, for it happens to the all of us that are to be allowing of our true essence to be seen within. It is within this voice of asking that these words are to appear to weigh heavy within the many of you that are to realize to ask.

WHAT AM I?
WHO AM I? WHERE AM I?

No matter the arrangement of these words they are still to be realized as the awakening of ones innerness within yourself that is to be realized to be in the wanting of, to remember of all that she is to be.

It is in your allowing of these words to be asked to be heard that one must start to search as you would see it in your own understanding of, for it is to be of such an opportunity within you to hear of this question. Although one that often leads yourself into much despair and hardship of which it is to fear the answering of this question to be not of your knowing.

In the quietest of moments that you are to allow for in your busyness that you so often refuse to allow to quieten outside of you. This nagging of this WHO AM I becomes louder and more prevalent to ones such as you in the further searching of the answer to which it is that you are looking for.

The quest we like to inform you of is this that it appears within the physical form of which you are is not the external searching of WHO IT IS THAT YOU ARE, for although it feels like this. The true understanding of which if you are allowing of yourself to stand with us as the guiders to you of all that you are to search for, this answer that is struggling to rise within so that it can be finally heard is the eternalness of which it is that you are in the becoming of to be.

YES! We agree easier said than done when you are to inhabit this heavy external form of matter that you are contained within. It is in this knowing of lightness that is you from within that reaches to the heavens to further afield that this asking is to become your knowing of.

It is to advise you that this knowledge is to be asked for it to be given. This we offer to you to know of which it is that you are to do so of, but in your inability to be hesitant to the quiet that is you internally to be found, this is where ones such as you are to be allowing of this answer to be found.

When you are in the space to ask of this question and let it be known that it appears out of nowhere for some, for it is your true reminder of all that you were asking of in the becoming of you that you are to be that it becomes known to you. In the allowing of this to be answered much internal shifting and realigning of the physical, emotional, mental and existing being that you are to have thought of,

WHO IT IS THAT YOU ARE.

Is to be undermined to a degree of self-doubting, regret, fear of the unknown to be, hatred of oneself in the understanding of this new you, this hatred and disappointment that is to become of you for the interruption and let us inform you it will feel like a shake up or a disruption from all that you thought it was that you were.

For it is your time of arising that it is allowed to be heard from your inner being that is to be of the asking to know that you are in the space to hear. You as many we have observed to understand will and are in the continual process of the shoving down, the numbing of, the inability to hear this feeling of WHO IT IS THAT YOU ARE that is rising from deep within you, this is the truest you that is to be seen, to be felt for she is in the prime positioning of time within this now that you are to reside within to hear of, to ask for.

Let's offer to you this understanding of what it is that you are, for many we have followed and been aware of their ability to know of this. The answer is within you if you are to listen to hear. For the greatness that is you that is to be discovered within you, YES! Greatness, this is for you to hear for it is in this greatness that you are to accept as your own then it is on the path of discovering of THE ALL THAT I AM TO BE will be realized. For those of you that are willing to listen to the calling whispers or of the loud roar that it will surely become if left to long on the burner so to speak, this path of openness to the internal being that is you to stand within for in this understanding of to hear.

You will know that the answer to this question so often asked truly is WHO YOU ARE IS YOU!

In the knowing of this that you are to be you and the many that are to passionately search. It is to be offered to you that in your continual external searching of those and that of which it is that may hold the answer for you, let us be able to offer to you to know. This they do not and nor will they.   For it is to be seen as an inner experiment that is to be undertaken by those that are serious enough about the disturbance this asking of WHO AM I has caused.

For it is in the disturbance of your outside life parse and your internal understanding of that which is attached to the physical body of all that you be in this life.

We offer to you here that it is in this disturbance that you will start to feel the rumbling deep within you, to allow for this eruption to become your inner journey of discovering of all that you are to be realized into.

For you, much work in the heart space opening of this that you are as an eternal being first and foremost is to begin.

It is in this journeying of discovering the one that you are that is to be the ultimate goal by those of you that undertake this magnificent understanding of ones such as you.

It is to be sought out within you with much reasoning of the logical mind to want to understand of this that you are becoming, for it is not of the logical mind that you are to ask.

For it is to be allowed to simplify all that you are to ask of it? For your trueness is the thinker in this situation and you will be encouraged to think in this space of thought often and more predominately. It is a must to those that are searching of this that they are asking of themselves to find the answer, to resist the urge that the physical outer realms of Mother Earth puts upon oneself.

You are to search within for this discovery must take place within this being that you are, it is to start here within this NOW that you are. In the searching of the answers externally you no doubted will be meet with much hindrance towards the real answer to be allowed to be heard. For you as humans are adjusted to this distant rumbling of sound that is to fill your physical ability to hear of what it is that surrounds you. This we must ask of you to allow for this to fall away to allow for the true noises of which it is that you are to hear.

In this we offer the sound of the true noises are very simply to be written here to offer, it is to be the sound of your breathe and your beating heart to slow to the sense of all that you are in the power of to become. These are the true voices of which are to whisper to you the way inward.

One must allocate allotted dedicated time within their understanding of what it is that they are to call their schedule within the physical day. It is that they simply must adjust this schedule of which we see so many of you to pack and jam as much into to be never quite accomplished. Thus allowing for the thoughts of the next day to be even fuller to the extreme of which the physical body becomes overwhelmed. In the creation of this space for your thoughts to be gathered and by this we mean, to be allowed to be left to chance for no recognition of which it is that you are thinking is desired by us, to allow for your transformation of this that you are to become.

It is often and most likely that all that you are needing to hear is to be allowed to unravel within you so as to be informed of the searching to cease within. This process is to be thought of as a slow meandering trail for you to cherish to which it is to be experienced, for it is your trail of discovering the being that you are that is to be allowed to be seen by you. In the unfolding of all that you hold within you in this space of discovering.

You must never power ahead in this practice of intention that you do for the quietness is what is to evoke the religious aspect to this offering of which it is that you are in the process of preforming. We do not offer specifics towards this that you undertake for all that you are is to be realized by you and not in the form of another's offering to you.

Know that you will be ever guided by your intuitiveness that is to be your true essence of within that you are so in the arrival time to the beginning of this to be, it is for you to realize that in this searching of the beginning, it has already begun to be.

One must be gentle upon themselves in this space that you are to create for it is here within the external you, the physical you, the ego you, loves to take over all that you are to be for it is in the I know right of all that you think that you are.

This is where we are to lose many of you that are trying to make head of this that you are wanting to participate into. It is the physical form, the emotional form that you are that is to offer you many thoughts here in this space. This is where we ask of you to remain steadfast to the truth and still within yourself, for it is in your deeper knowing that is to be within you that you are to feel the true worth of your knowing that is yours to be heard.

Allow the senses to soften so that you may fall into a place of gently persuasion of this as a pleasant, easy place to dwell within. For it takes time here to be with all that is to be busy outside and internally within the physical form that you are. You will find the struggles of this asking that you are attempting to become, to rise to the surface very quickly, so that it is to be fought with the inability in your thinking of this that you cannot do.

We offer here to you with much LOVE for you to feel, to hear that it is in this trying of that we witness the many of you doing, that it is being done and it is to be heard to offer to you, that you are surrounded in this space of you with the love that is to be felt by you. If it is only in this love that you feel then you are succeeding within this first of many attempts to be in your quietness to hear of us.

For in these first attempts that you are to make and this we offer there are to be many for the ability to go from 100-0 in one session is virtually impossible to obtain.

But it is shown for those of you that are able to sit in practiced quiet of the inner being it is to be known that you will find the quiet of the physical being that you are searching for. This physical being has been the most important part of who you thought it was or is that you are. It will offer you much struggle to this that you are thinking of trying to undertake, to be of in the ability to listen to the true essence of you that has until now laid quietly dormant and unheard within you. This is to be felt as an unusual shift in thinking patterns for you to undertake, so allow for your inner kindness and calm thoughts to be revealed to you to flourish within, so all that you are asking of can be heard.

> *IN THE TRUENESS OF WHO YOU REALLY ARE INTO THE BECOMING OF, IS WHERE YOUR GREATEST ASSESTS WILL BE FOUND FOR THEY ARE YOU, THIS INNERNESSS THAT IS TO BE REALISED AS THE TRUE YOU THAT YOU ARE. EMBRACE ALL THAT YOU BE.*

The feelings of self-doubt and inability to attain this space that so many of you speak of as the place to be. It is to be known to you to be always in your ability of to sit within in the timing of which it is that you are to find it to be yours, for there are many, yes we offer this to you to hear that there are many able to answer this questioning of their entirety of.

"WHO IT IS THAT THEY ARE".

But one is to remember here that it is in their becoming of this that they are that they became, for you are to realize that in your becoming of this that you are becoming you already are.

For one will never stand in such total place of achieving of all that it is that they are to be, for in this that we offer to you to know that it is ever evolving into the bigger being that you are striving within to be.

Your personal growth & self-knowing within is to surpass all limitations that you feel are placed upon you by your own self doing in your inability to achieve of this that you are asking. This is to be allowed to fray away from you for you are to stay strong in your quest to desire of this true being that you are searching. She will be found within you, to hear you to speak and to rise up to offer to you this magnificent lightness that you are to be yet discovered into.

> *IN ONES SEARCHING OF, THERE WILL ALWAYS BE OF SOMETHING TO BE FOUND.*

In the ability to shift ones thinking from the mundane to the imaginary than this is a great stepping stone to be able to realize of all that is available in this space of opening to you. For it is in this imagination that is yours and no it does not have to be big, fancy or affluent but to be asked of is more the asking it should be able to be envisioned into. For in this space of delving into, you will inherit the urges to adjust yourself within a space of outer regions that are far from the mundaneness that appears to be offered to you within the normal understanding of quiet space to think.

Imagination is your greatest asset as we see it to offer to you to understand of this ability for quietness to overcome you in the ability to slip away from the earthly realms so to speak of inner thoughts. This is to be a place that you and the many that are trying to find this position within themselves of quiet can be found to suit you exactly as it is asked of you to be.

MINDFUL EXERCISE:

In this moment is your NOW!

This is to be thought of as an exercise for those that are to begin, it is in this process that the beginning of your quiet space is to be allowed to enter into your daily activities of to do list.

This is the place that it will grow into astronomical proportions of desiring of all that you are asking of to be found to be here.

For it is here that there are no limits, no misunderstandings from another, no inabilities to find of what it is that you are asking. It is in your knowing to know that you must just go along with the space that is being opened within you to sit. No judgement placed on or of what is allowed to rise to desire of to see.

In the desiring of this space to open more and more of which it will, it becomes a space of contentment to be, a space of innermost love that is to grow in passion and grace for all that you are receiving. It is strong within here that you feel for you are able to sit within your thoughts of nonchalant that are emerging into you to be allowed to be discovered to be adventurous within.

This space is yours for the asking of, this is your space that you have found and are in the new habit of creating. So we ask of you to sit firstly and always in love, then let the doors swing open so to speak to allow for the emerging of this space to be completely designed by your innerness that is us in the guiding of you to be.

It is offered to you here to realize, to know that much internal dialogue and emphasis is placed upon this physical form in the asking of what it is that they are needing to know. For if you are to realize that all that you are in the needing of to know is etched within this innerness that is yet to be allowed to speak.

So do not dwell internally and in self-conflicting intentions of this that you are not in the place yet of to receive.

As it appears to the asking of others to be progressing for it is to be remembered that it is entirely into you that this asking is to be held, it will not be raised by another this you must know.

Often the path of self-doubt is the path to your internal beings demise of being discovered, allow her to speak within you this you will hear as your own voice of understanding of reason to be heard.

For she speaks differently to you this appears to be heard by you, for she only speaks with love and in this love that she speaks is the true way of knowing that you are in the connection of all that she is to be speaking of in truth for you to realize into.

In the inner power-ness that is yours to be discovered and we use this word to describe of what it feels like within, in a human understanding of this that has been relayed to us.

In the many that we have found their feedback to be useful in the describing of this that you are attempting to understand as your own.

In your power is you! This is to be seen as an opening of such within you that does not allow for the ego within that is to be seen as your purpose of this to be discovered, for it is not so.

The power that is to be attached to this greatness that we speak of so often.

In this greatness that you are to stand within so that your heart space may burst open in this offering to us from you so that it is known by us that it is in your true desiring of this to be discovered within you that it shall be offered.

It is to be offered here that no untruths of you that you are asking of can be offered in this space and the time that you have allocated to this exact timing of which it is that it will be realized within you, will be felt by you. And it is in this time only that the true understanding of this that you are searching for to discover within you will it be found.

YES; we offer here that it is in the true standing in which it is that you are to offer will all be felt for us to hear, of this we ask of you to know, that it was in your decided asking of, that it will be realized to you. One is not to appear to be in a hurry for this chosen path of yours has been asked for in the embryo of discovering of this that you were in the becoming of.

So you will be wise to wait patiently in the receiving as it unfolds and to always enjoy of what it is that you are feeling to see, to sense. For this is your story that is being revealed to you and much is to be undertaken by you before your true path is revealed within you to walk upon.

We speak here to those of you that are just in the beginning of such an asking of. This is to feel like an unsuspecting stance within yourself that you are undertaking, for it is to be realized to be said that this inner contentment that we speak of here that is yours to be discovered will not come without a fight.

This we know to offer, for the strength of the human component that is yours to decide within yourself is strong in the many of you that are in the process of trying to evolve into this asking of this that has been heard within you.

DO NOT DESPAIR.

For it is achievable to all that are to remain committed. This commitment is to be felt within you firstly, for it is to be addressed by your thoughts of logic first. This we understand to offer and this is the place of contempt that the issues surrounding your inner release is attached to.

So in this we offer that it is your ability to want for this so deeply to be felt, that it will be in your asking of this we attach to you the scenario of at first if one does not succeed one must try again for it is in the trying of that it becomes in the ability of to do.

For the most of you this is to be seen as a task of never had to do before and in this awakening within you that it is to be known by those of you that have experienced it to the degree in which love will overtake your every waking thoughts. Too often then in this task to think of, it impacts ones thoughts as of a hardship or chore. This we wish it not to be thought of as such. For if it is to become this way of thinking, one must rest their physical form to the extent of in the ability to try again in the next scheduled time slot that is to be allocated to this form of physical interaction within the innerness that is yours to be heard.

We ask of you to allow for all thoughts associated with the ideals of what you are to call meditation to be released by you. It is to remove all this that you understand that is to be offered to you by the many that are in the position to think that they are helping you in your progression of this to be found. It is not of their path that is to be followed by you. You must only allow firstly yourself to be able the time to sit within the quiet that is to be recognized as yours, if elements of material matter such as music, water or flames from candles are to be needed to find a fixing point within you, than let this be by your own discovery for it is not of another's ability or path that this is to be shown to you.

This is to be your journey of discovery and the true you that is to be heard will be your ever efficient guider inwardly to the outward realms that you are to transpire within. For it is seen as an ancient understanding of this that is to be known as meditation by those of you that are to partake within this space that we like to call;

> *The sitting within your true being so that the pure consciousness that you are of is to be always heard.*

To allow for oneself to be recognized as the being that she is to be, is the greatest understanding of which it is that you will undertake in this lifetime upon this planet that you are to stand upon. For it is in your power of discovering of this your journey will be even more advanced into the next realms of understanding. To become into the newest being of deciding of all that you so choose to be in the asking of to become. Never allow for the complacent feelings of lack of this love to be established within you by another, for your true inner finding is to be able to sit strong at most within you. This we offer for in this strength is your becoming into the love that you are all in the asking of to be allowed to be recognized into this that you are. For in here is your answer to your becoming.

ALL THAT I AM.

CHAPTER TWO

IN LOVE IT IS THAT I SIT

It is this love that is to always dwell within ones such as yourself to sit into, most often it is the inability to see of this love that be you to see, that often leads to the feeling of such a lack of love that you are to be to be found.

The innermostness that is you to be heard for she is in love first and foremost with you this you are to know. For the love that is to be developed or rather allowed to be developed within yourself is the hardest of loves to establish, to find, to hear, for this love has and is to be known as the love that has been neglected by the many of you that have been in search for this love that is to be yours in this lifetime and all that you are choosing to interact within.

This love is the grandest love on offering for you; for this love is you, this love is the inner being that is offering this love to you for it is not of another's love that it is to be felt to be received, for it will not and cannot compare to this love that you will find within the true searching and to allow to be heard that is yours within.

It is cliché that we offer these words to hear, for it is the hardest journey that many of you will undertake and those of you that have found this love, whom of which have connected into this love, will always still be searching for more of this love that is limitless in its offering of to you. For this is the love that is to fill you to overflowing and in the opening of this love within oneself, one must realize that this love is never to be ending. So that you will always stand in this recognition of this love that is yours, it flows so evanescently from us to you from the creator of all that be.

It is to be the greatest gift that ones such as yourself can give to yourselves in all times of contemplation and quiet times to acknowledge of this love. For it is all yours to receive and in the receiving of this love it is to be allowed to be given so intently from within you, to all that you are to stand within, for it has no choice but to flow forth.

Upon you're asking to find this love, to allow for it to be realized within you this is the easy path. For it is also to be found in others in their searching for they too are wanting to find of this love and it is in this love that the lure of it to be found casts a spell upon you so to speak. For once its flow has been allowed to be established there is to be no hesitation of this to flow unto all that you are to be in the presence of.

There is to be no thinking of how to do this or what of to do.

It is a natural understanding within those of you that are in the discovery of this that is to be called the 'power of love' that sits divinely within you. For this love is not to be held back in any way of understanding of for there is nothing to understand of this that you feel. It is to be exactly as it appears for in its pure path that it is to enter you, it too will find its true path of exiting to the surroundings that it is to find itself within.

Love such as this is thought of as such a humbling feeling to be able to experience. This you are to know, to hear that it is not to be humble in this love. For all that you are needing to be feeling is within you in the first place to allow for this love to be ignited intensely within you.

Stop all the human emotions to describe of what it is that you feel that you are to allow for this love, it is to be known that these emotions, feelings are so intertwined divinely encrypted within this feeling of love that it is not to be thought of as a doing. It is not this love that is yours to allow for the flowing into and out of that is to be yours, so allow always to not offer thought of it for it is already within you to be.

Yes! This love is different in offering to you than of what it is that you are to experience externally given to you by another. For in this love that you are all to crave, we see to witness of in another it is held with such a regret and a wanting of at the same time. For in this external love that is not yours to give, it is to be received so that another knows of their self-worth in your eyes which we wish to eliminate these thoughts of love to be thought of like this.

For if you are to see your love as the biggest first than you are not in need of another's love to be seen by your physical eyes to feel that you are in fact loved.

Allow for your love for yourself to overrule any of this love that you are searching of to be offered to you by another.

It is not of theirs to give, for they are to first find the love within themselves and then it shall be felt to be offered, but not to be given. For in the giving of this external love sits much despise for the asking of it to be received of another so that one must feel as though they are needing to give to be on the receiving end of this love you see.

> *Love as we offer to you to see it, to feel it,*
> *(Insert your name here).*

This LOVE is to be the most extravagant and the most uplifting and most humbling of emotions that one is to ever experience. For to go through life as it is that you are to know of it to be without this kind of love is to be in the inability of us to foresee it to arise, for it is in this love that one is to hold within themselves that this sense of release to breathe and this sense of freedom that is to rise from and the ability to sit within ones worthiness of all that you are.

If you are to be able to look inwardly into the being of which it is that is to hold this love for you in the waiting of for you to realize it that it is of yours to discover. Then in this asking of this love to be found within you then and only then can you begin your path of self-awareness into the being of which it is that you are born out of.

For the love that rages so fiercely here within us is to be seen in all of its worthiness, its offering of this to you is to be understood by you that you are of this love. This is the complete love that is to be found inside of you.

YOU ARE THIS LOVE THAT WE SPEAK OF.

In the getting to know oneself and in disregarding all that does not suit you in the negative understanding of which it is interpreted as to be spoken to you by yourself or another. It is to be allowed for this nonsense talking to be washed away, for in the true sense of the being that is the love within you, will not tolerate this to be the speech in which it is that you are to get side tracked into.

For this love that prevails all within you is too big to be caught up in this nonsense of negating talk of that, which is not true within you that you are.

Allow for this that she is to hold this love to rise gently and ever so softly within you, for she is in the understanding of the place that you so stand in. It saddens her to know of this place that you see yourself is not one of self-worth or of a faithful understanding to trust, for this was never meant to be of you that denies this love internally. For it was asked from you to always burn with such power and desire within you to always see yourself in this strength of which it is that you are becoming into once more.

In this realization of this love, it is to become a journey of quiet contemplation and most importantly of self-allowing of this to evolve within you. For we see this in so many of you this lost feeling towards this love that is yours always to receive.

In the ability that you have possessed upon this earth to feel in the human aspect of yourself, you have also allowed for this powerful love that is yours to go unnoticed eventually realizing into this that you are not to approve of. So allow for this voice of little love to grow slowly, ever so steadily towards your heart space, for this is of where you will feel her first. She is tentative in her offering for it is known by us that the many of you that have lost this love and trust within yourself is yet to allow for it to open again once more into the becoming of what it always is to be a part of.

BEGIN IN YOUR CLOSENESS OF YOURSELF TO TRUST THE WORDS OF GENTLE CALM THAT ALTHOUGH MAY BE HARD TO VOICE OR UTTER. FOR IT IS IN THE MIND NOT OF THE SEEER OR SAYING THAT IT IS TO FIRST BE ALLOWED TO START. TRUST THAT SHE LIKES OF YOU WAY MORE THAN OF WHAT YOU DO OF YOURSELF IT IS TO BE OFFERED. FOR IT IS IN THIS KNOWING OF YOU THAT YOU WILL ALLOW HER WORDS TO SIT UPON YOUR SKIN DELICATELY FOR THAT IS TO BE THE HOLD THAT YOU ARE NEEDING TO FEEL RIGHT NOW.

Be prepared for the internal fight that is to be won over and over again by the human mind that does not care for you like you think. It is this grey matter that is to rule your thoughts of distrust so often and is not in it to become friends, for it has a role to play and this role must be won at all costs.

This grey giant of the human form that is to appear to be smarter than your heart, this is to be heard today that it is not.

Once the heart is to be opened to this love that is yours to own once again and to the love that is to fill it so creatively, then this giant that is to overrule your thoughts of the perfection that you sit within then and only then will the heart win. Although it is not the nature of the heart to think of this as a competition, for it knows only in love it is that it is to always win over the unjust that is so often offered to those in war.

The cursor to this love that is to be so prevalent upon its finding is that no other love will be felt as grand and in this offering to you it is to be known that this love is you.

Whimsical this may sound but your heart is the real adventurer that lays within for it is in her opening of to this love that is to be found, to be allowed to enter in your asking of it to be, then in this love is where you will find yourself to stand.

At first she is to allow for you to feel naked and raw and as torn as to of what it is to be felt of this love.

It then settles into an understanding of this that could be available to you if you are to follow the offerings that are to be given. Then the down ward turn of distrust enters, for it appears as though it is not of a trueness that this love can and could be felt so raw like this in its power of knowing you at your best and worst without judgment.

This then leads into the trials and tribulations of judgement that we hang upon ourselves like scarfs for everyone to take notice of.

> *'AM I JUSTIFIED OR WORTHY ENOUGH TO BE IN THIS PLACE I STAND IN LOVE',*

Then comes the tender most moment of them all… when you fall to your knees in the deepest of humbleness's, into the feelings of lack of yourself to deserve this love that you are to feel. Then in the hereafter of this to feel, you will discover that it is your love for you that you have been searching for and are now capable to allow it to saturate you from within. So that it ebbs from within you like a gentle outpouring of warmth to heal, comfort and fill this physical being of love that holds you and to be felt by all that are to encounter you.

This is your love, the love that you are to embrace yourself now in this realization of this into your becoming of.

This is the searching that so many of you are in the process of undertaking, know it will be found for it is always yours to feel. Allow for this realization of this that you are to bring tears to your eyes, to break even the strongest of exteriors and to undo much if not all of the untruths that you have held within oneself as to be real.

It is in the physical reals of this love that has been deceived into staying hidden and out of view so as not to be spoken of or asked to be heard, that these tears are to flow.

In the transforming of oneself into a space of allowing one must always see the tears as the well of desire that has been boarded over so as not to be allowed to be felt.

This well is strong within you, its light that shines within it is dull often to the first seeing of, but as the tears of love start to flow this well begins to empty so that the light that is within you can fill this well to the brightness of which it is now being called to shine.

This lightness and love opens your heart space within to the Love that is to be known as your BIG LOVE that is yours to be heard, to be eternally felt.

WHEN ONE IS TO FEEL SUCH OF THIS LOVE WITHIN THEMSELVES, IT IS LIKE A REMINDER FROM WITHIN TO BE SEEN TO BE REMEMBERED, THAT THIS IS THE LOVE THAT FILLS YOU COMPLETELY, WITH NO ASKING OF TO BE OFFERED INTO.

CHAPTER THREE

MY BIG LOVE

One is to sit in wonderment and awe, and if we are honest maybe a little confusion, of this love that is now to be realized within themselves. For this love is to be allowed into your existence in the exact moment of realization of it to be offered.

HOW DO I FIND THIS BIG LOVE WITHIN ME? WHEN I DON'T FEEL LOVE FOR MYSELF AT ALL.

Yes! We do offer to you that it is not that you do not love of yourself, it is in the continual hiding away of this love, the frightened feelings of attachment to this love that are forgotten and that you have become suppressed inwardly to the feeling of this love that is yours to cherish within.

For often in much consideration towards others that are to offer you interaction from birth to your current NOW of which it is that you are participating within. It is to be felt this loss of such as the love that you are to realize as yours. For in these constant interactions both asked for and freely given is the ability within oneself to take on-board all that is to be offered to them to receive. This we must ask of you to know that this is not to be so. Leave all offerings open ended so to speak so that they may flow into but most importantly through you as you are to stand before them.

These offerings are not of yours to undertake or hold within for this is not your BIG Love speaking to and offering you words that you are in the need of to hear, it is not.

Your BIG LOVE words of yours are to appear in perfect timing of which it is that you are to desire of them to be. These big love words from within you are brave, bold, gentle, encouraging and blissfully rewarding to the inner being that you are to be.

So allow for this BIG LOVE that wells up inside of you to prove a point within you that you are capable to live, breathe and step into this big love. For it is yours this you are to know to receive. It is not of another to hear these silent whispers or loud roars of this big love that is speaking. It is to be heard only by you and in your allowing for the resistance to slip away at what you hear being spoken of from another, then and only then will you stand a little taller, grow a little prouder, sing louder, dance more and show the world that is to witness the unfolding of this that is you to blossom into and resume being the blessed being that you were destined to be.

Here is where you will find your BIG LOVE that is to adore you, to offer to you the real person of you that you are to BE. Trust in the powerfulness that is starting to swell inside of you, this you will feel as a reluctant receiving of this LOVE that wants to be felt, to receive of, for it is in this asking to be offered to you that it is to be offered. One must be willing to allow for such a transformation to be undertaken almost as if it is to be allowed to unfold within themselves without the attention that one would think is needed.

In the ability to just allow for it to rise up within it self you will feel it flourish within you to be seen to be felt. There are to be no needs attached to this love, for in this to offer it is often the hardships that are attached to your earthly love that one applies to the BIG LOVE that is theirs to be in possession of. In this big love is your understanding of a want to be the love that you are holding onto inside, let it be free to flourish and to escape from within you. Let it be spoken that it is not of another that is to help guide you in this transformation of love, only you are to be the offeror to oneself to be in the place of too desire this BIG LOVE, to be able to sit within so that it is to awaken all of which it is that you are.

LOVE.

BIG LOVE is felt in so many different ways for each and every one that is in their asking of it to be received. It reveals to you in your commitment to oneself and those that are to be seen as your ever-loving support and guides to all that is. In this we offer to you all to hear of this that we are always wanting of this the biggest love for you to be. For in this big love is the being of love and light that you are to be seen by us eternally. We sit in the grace and the unfolding of all that you are to relish within you. For this love though it is yours, it is your bigness to offer this to yourself that sets you apart from all of those other internally powered offerors shining their own unique BIG LOVE to be seen by you.

Channeled offering to receive in regards to these writings of

THE BIG LOVE THEORY.

Big love is not of such that we are to see it, as this that you are portraying it to be. In this that you are calling big love is much to be thought of. It is in this love that yes is big for a word for you to describe it as being. This is to be known to be heard that this love is ours to offer to you upon your realizing of this that you are to ask. For the many that are asking to be found within this love must be willing to do the work so to speak of entering into oneself. So as to untie all inhabitations and attachments that one holds within themselves to be allowed to be seen to offer.

Ones journey within allows for much evolving into this that they are to despise at times. Often they are met with hindrances and unforgettable moments within this life that they are in need of dealing with to begin the process of inner healing as you would call it. It is in your human understanding that one must be a clear and clean channel to offer to us that it will be revealed to you the destiny of which it is that you are searching of.

One such as your self's are to always be reminded here in this your Now of hearing that you are always in the correct positioning of which it is to be clear and clean as to speak of as to receive into their perfection all that is to be you.

This we offer to know, that it is in you asking of this love to be yours that it will be yours, for it is this you are to know.

It is already within you, implanted within you deeply so that it would not be forgotten of. It is in the ability of the human understanding of emotions such as sadness, hatred, grief, ignorance of self and guilt that many layers are allowed to be thrown over this love that is.

It is for me to ask, why is it that we do this?

We feel it is to offer yourself an understanding of protection outwardly to the demands that the many of you are sitting within in this life that is yours to ask for. These demands appear to be a heavy burden to carry and are just as you see them to be. This they are as you are to realize them into your existence of this that you are. Allow for these burdens to be downgraded and emptied outwardly for they are not of you to carry, they are not in existence of, if you are to allow for your minds to be not negotiable to this that you think of as a burden.

So we offer, to ones such as you that are searching for the big love as you are to call it, YES, it is of a bigness that is overwhelming and feels almost unachievable to those of you that are looking for it at times. Because many of you are functioning within the human form that you are most in awareness of and are easily led by self or others to criticize those that are in this space. Without any hesitation into the way in which it is. Many of you are to justify the guilt, jealousy even unworthiness that you hold within yourselves for the feelings that you feel inwardly and outwardly of seeing another just simply being of this BIG LOVE.

This is why it is that you are unwillingly blocking yourself to be in this position within to except this big love as yours.

It is to offer here that if you are to allow for all that be, to be able to be of themselves, it is then in your understanding and ability to feel into this same

BIG LOVE.

So… YES this big love, is the ultimate place to stand into. This big love as it is to be called by you, it is the place of pure consciousness that we are to be seen, to be felt. In this big love is us that are so in the wanting for you all to open up to your hearts asking of not to be forgotten of this big love that you are here and willing to be. So that we may enter into this space of co-alignment within all that we are to be for you to see, to feel once again. We are of this big love that you and the many that are searching for and it is in us that this Big love is to be found in all of its truth and desires that are to be yours to ask.

In my wanting to feel this Big Love, are there any suggestions in regards to the allowing of it to be?

Often in want there is to be felt resistance, for in the wanting of what it is that one feels they do not have there lays the resistance to the having of.

One is to be genuine in one's heart space opening and in time this will be revealed to you of an understanding of what this is to be felt like from within. To share of this space within you that is to be always in the deepest understanding of the love for you is to be in a space of complete allowing.

It is to be seen as your space of remembrance of all that you are to be in witness of to become. The heart space is yours to feel open in any time you are asking of it to be. This we will establish within you in the upcoming pages to be read to feel within.

In the ability of one to see themselves capable to love of oneself in this Big Love fashion, one is to first be allowed to be complete within themselves and their own understanding of which it is that you are.

It is not to see yourself in the eyes of another, for it does not appear to help on this seeing of yourself in a true way.

They will never be in this position of you to be, to be able to see yourself as the believer that you are of the being that you are within. It is this that is to be the first most noticeable change within that you must undertake.

To allow for this transformation within so that you may witness significant change, allow for yourself to be loved by you and to be the recipient of this big love, for it is yours for the taking. Watch on as the human aspect of you fights and disagrees with this contentiousness of resisting of which it is that you are offering to be heard. For this my dears is the first step onto your path of finding your own big love that is yours to cherish from within once again.

Consideration is needed here to be heard that this internal dialogue that is so prevalent to the hearing of it to be offered by self. It is to be diligent to the unwillingness of the self to be in the position to be in a stance that is strong enough to challenge its offerings in any way.

This we offer. You will, for your confidence if allowed to, will grow in its willingness to be heard, to be wanted to develop within for it is the smallest of accomplishments that are to become prominent from within this that is you. This is the place that you will stand defiant to that voice of despair, this voice of not enough, lack of, it is no longer needed to be heard by you.

It is to be seen that you are in the becoming a willing participant into the finding of this Big Love that is yours to find. Feel as it is to saturate you with feelings of such joy, love and offering resilience to the outside world and all that are to betray you in a sensing of this that you are becoming into . This you that has found her voice to hear, to know of and to allow for it to choose your words that are in need to be spoken in truth of this Big Love that is lovingly supported in the all that you are to be of.

Will we ever feel worthy and allowing of, to be the holders of this BIG LOVE?

If and when one is able to be honest in their listening of all that is to be spoken of from the beholder of all that is correct and right within them.

Then and only then will you as the asker of this BIG LOVE, feel your worthiness to be of.

Will it be in your ability to receive freely of this love that is to be so knowing of you in this form that you are to be asking of, that in here you are to feel of all that we are in our ever loving ability of love to give to you? For it is in this that we see so many of you to think of it to be a gift to you. This we must correct, it is not of gifting that it is to be thought of, it is to be known as a strong-ness within you that this is pure love, that is so complete and of such within you that it is this BIG LOVE that is yours to ask for and own and be willing to live once more into this that you are to be surrounded into.

CHAPTER FOUR

ALLOWING OF THE UNFOLDING WITHIN

To be in the place to witness your own unfolding is a place of great stance within, so that you will be in the willingness to be this that you are of wanting to be.

To witness your unfolding of all that you are hiding within is to be such a greatness to be able to cherish. For in the unfolding is much love, encouragement of and ability to see yourself for the being of which it is that you are destined to be. We see you all standing proudly from within for this is the true place one is to stand. But it is in the allowing of the human that you are to undertake and give into this as the governing ruler within you, this is where the layers begin to hinder all that you seek to be.

Much is to be offered here to speak with you of, it is to be seen as an unfolding for the fact of which it is to sit within you this need to be of something that of which it is that you are not.

In the searching of this your I AM, we are to witness in the many of you that this is to be allowed to be changed so undecidedly by you in the format of others that are to offer much to you in the thinking of which it is that you are to think that you are or need to be.

When we speak of unfolding as such, it is to realize that in this we offer the un-layering of all the layers that are within you. These layers have been layered consistently within you in the spoken or unseeing sense that someone or circumstance of situations has made you feel as though you are of not what is it that you really are.

So layer upon layer has been allowed to be accepted into your physical sensation of this that you perceive yourself to be. From birth to your current NOW that you are to sit in here, is the layering that you are feeling of, it has been left unattended in the many of you for much of your time here upon this planet. In this we see it as a throwing over or dulling down of this inner being of which it is that you are, so that she is almost unrecognizable to the seeing inner eye of this that you are to respond to.

For she has been allowed to sink so deeply within you that this light that is yours is not illuminating of its space that it dwells. In this layering, is where the unfolding of you the inner you is to commence. It often is to start as a suggestion by you or maybe of another, more often than not it is in your own realizing of, that you are ready to hear of this unfolding.

As in this very moment of which it is that you are sitting in your NOW to read this page.

For it is written only for you to hear in such time that you are ready to begin this process of to unfold.

In this unfolding it is to be described as like a game of pass the parcel at a child's birthday party, for each layer of wrapping has been placed there to purposely cover the one underneath, so this is the way in which the layering of oneself is to begin in the first instance. By the placing of another layer over the one that is to exist in hope of hiding all that does not serve you away out of sight so that it does not need to be seen to be realized by the eyes that are looking inwardly.

So as each layer is recognized, allowed and asked of to be removed of which it is in perfect time as the game allows for it to be with music attached.

We see this in your physical form that a different scenario or meditative session of quiet contemplation, course or conversation that strikes a tune within you is in the perfect timing of which your innerness that is speaking to you is heard. Then and only then is another layering of the inner light of which is hidden, allowed to be removed.

Each layer into this unfolding of what it is that you are inside is the true you, each layer represents to you physical emotions, negative thoughts, comments by another or yourself or neglect experienced to be revealed attached to this layer.

It allows for you to recognize within you that there is to be another more exuberant you, if you keep unfolding and letting these layers to be allowed to be lifted to be removed.

Some layers are heavier or denser than others and they may take a little more time and human effort for you to unwrap to be opened. This is okay, for not all that has been placed there was attached to another. Many of these layers begging to be allowed to be unfolded are sitting in this space within you because of your own doing, and you yourself are the best layers of issues that need to be hidden within yourself.

It is of the human aspect that one is to think that one must push down these emotions, thoughts, feelings to hide them inwardly and that this is the best way to ignore of what it is that we do not wish to deal with so that it cannot be seen outwardly anymore.

Be kind in this unfolding of, for it is not always felt as a place of a sunny reveal. For more often than not it is to be a dark, gloomy place to sit within whilst the papers of the unfolding are getting sorted and folded to be allowed to be removed from the hidden aspects, so that they can be accepted by oneself as to be offered unto us in the rawness of it is that they are to be felt.

We establish within you to hear this, that in the unfolding of and the removal of these layers that there will be many issues that are to have human emotions or names attached to, such as hurt, guilt, lost loves, worthlessness, fears and indecisions of all that you thought that you were.

These are to be allowed to be seen as simply this, not of who it is that you are to be. They are all layers of a time and space that you were not in the correct alignment or hearing of which it is that you are.

It is often in one's human form that it is easier to cover up and hide than to go inside within to realize that the truthful you is the only way to ease these moments that have simply been trapped within. Only to then need a layering of such so that they cannot be seen to be felt any longer by you the holder.

The complete truth of the matter that we see often within your human experience is to allow oneself to feel numb to the fact of what really is to be the true understanding of what it is to be felt.

It is the easier option for you to encourage within yourself the ignoring of this true rising of and recognition of what it is that you are to be.

This then allows yourself to feel disconnected to your higher self, so this you see is an innate ability that you as the human form has developed. Allowing oneself to move on from such pain of hurts, griefs and sadness's, to create a disillusion as such to sustain the façade outwardly that is to be thought of as needed to interact within society of today's normal personality standards.

Each layer as it is to be asked by you to be allowed to be unfolded is to be treated gently, for much humanism is attached to these folds and the correct timing is needed.

The correct acknowledgement into the timing of this is to be undertaken and if you are to listen to your intuitiveness of heart, which you all are in the power of owning then you will feel the correct timing within of this to become.

Each unfolding replicates an honesty within you that you are willing and that you are in the need of to be the true you that you are. Be brave for you must allow for all that swells within you as you steady yourself through this process.

It is to be known as the innermost being of which you are. That is being allowed to be heard once more to be felt.

In this process that we call the unfolding it is the true speaker within you that is to know of the process. For she has been your inner guider for many, many, many times over that you have undergone this process, and is in the habit of knowing the exact way in which it is to be undertaken.

Doubt should not be allowed to creep in for it will try to tell you that you are not in the correct position or not of worth enough in which to undertake this unfolding within, but we are to offer here that you are in the most perfect placement to begin to allow in this that is your now.

Watch as you become a great bystander to witness and your very own cheer squad to yourself for the layers that are allowed to be unfolded are softening as they are allowed to fall. It is in the sensing of the discovering of what it is that is to be found underneath all that has been hidden that is often to be felt as a driving force to be reckoned with once it is allowed to be witnessed to yourself to be seen to be felt.

One is to feel the removal of each layer as it falls away from the physical, emotional form, allowing for it to feel lighter, and clearer in a sense of feeling.

Appearing to offer a nakedness to oneself that may not have ever been felt before, for in the rawness of this unfolding leaves the self to feel vulnerable to the outside external wellbeing that is to resist of this that is in the process of being revealed.

The denser or older the layers, the deeper within it will be felt.

Most often as you allow for these layers to be unfolded this is when the hard work is to begin, for the more layers, the more inner work there is to be done in regards to your true self fighting for you to know the answer to the question so often asked.

WHO IS IT THAT I AM?

Let these layers be a gift to you as you feel them disintegrate to the ethers of all that will hold them for you, for this is to be seen as a removal of this that you are not.

So the deeper it is that one has to dig, the greater the prize at the end of this unfolding and revealing is to be found to be realized, and it is often felt with such an overwhelming sense of emotions attached with disbelief that one is to find themselves standing in.

For it has been a long time since you have allowed yourselves to see the true being of which it is that you are.

It is in this that we are to assist you. It is in the asking of this to begin that you will feel our presence, for it is always heard by us, but you must be in the place of hearing, to feel, to receive before this unfolding of yours is willing to begin. To be peeled away to open into the most beautiful, loving magnificent being that is yours to see, to feel again. It is in this unfolding much love is to be witnessed so that you will stand in your righteousness of this that you are, stake your claim to be in this that you stand and in here is where you are to feel to know,

THIS IS WHO I AM TO BE.

WHY IS IT THAT WE AS HUMANS FEEL THIS NEED TO LAYER OUR INNERNESS WITH THESE HIDDEN LAYERS?

When you as the true bearer truly believe of all that is correct and in wholeness of the All that is you, then and only then will you cease to offer this form of inner self neglect to yourself as an opportunity to better oneself in the eyes of another. So often this is seen to view by us.

We ask of you to recognize the All that is to be you, for you are all in the knowing of this inner wisdom that is solidly placed within you. It is in this knowing that your searching will cease, for it is in this asking from the innerness within that is to know all of you.

Here in lays your true being with no need to hide, for in your own truth and realizing of this that you are is the ability to recognize in truth before a layer as such to hide is to be placed.

For if you are always true to…

WHO IT IS THAT YOU ARE DESTINED TO BE,

The answers are always offered for you to hear. Although it isn't until you see yourself in this shining big love that is yours that you will remember of the All that is the perfect you that exists within.

All unfolding's are to be felt differently, for you are all so unique in each and every way and this is not to say that it is to be seen as separate from us. Though it is in us that we are to offer to you that in ALL that we are is to be you.

For we are fully unfolded with no layering in a sense to be needed. It is in our own Big love to recognize this as the trueness' in which it is that we stand ever present and ever guiding you towards this fulfilling, complete place of total openness so that you are to rejoice in all that you have experienced in your own personal unfolding.

May your inner being blossom always into her fullest potential, like the petals of a cherry blossom bud so that she may revel in the uniqueness that she is to experience, to feel the ease in which it is that you flower, never to be hidden under layers again. It is to be offered here that once the layers are allowed to float free, it is to be seen as the most unique reveal into this that you are to present.

CHAPTER FIVE

FINDING MY HEART SPACE

"In my Heart space I find you".

For it is this that you are to offer to me to receive as my truest understanding of which it is that I AM. For there is to be no other such as me and in this we offer to you to feel, the Love in us that you are to reside within, fully, completely and becoming of. The bliss that one is to realize within this space that we offer to you to be called as you do your heart space is to be the completeness in which one is to allow of themselves to be the wholeness of which it is that they are.

There is no need in this space to feel the pull of uncertainty towards that of which it is that you do not know. It is for you to know, all that you are to become into your becoming of, is within this space that generates such radiance of this love that is ours to offer to you to remember of this love once more.

Feel resonance of this space, for you are to remember it well upon your allowing of such space within to be opened.

In the depths of your understanding of all that you are is of this space that when it is to be opened into its fullest capacity of to receive, to flow, then and only then will you comprehend the readiness of which it is that you are to become.

In the confines that you as we offer to you to see, of which many of these confines are being held within you as distrust within yourself so that it may feel as though another is in control of all your thoughts, emotions and feelings many of which are to rise within yourself.

This is the strong pulling of dismissal within your ego or physical self that this love is not of importance enough within you to remember.

It is to be offered here to receive that it is often the ego and the physical form that do not respect the innerness of love at times within a trusting relationship to be true and of benefit to yourself. They will always be in the positioning of which it is to be concerned more of what it is that the physical form or ego personality is to gain by this want to be seen completely in this love that one searches for.

The challenge that we see within you to grasp and to acknowledge, is to be seen by the ego of oneself that the heart is to be a place of giving and receiving of love alongside another to be of something that is to be earnt or given.

This is incorrect for this heart space that you speak of is seen and felt only with the physical eyes of yours to offer its opinion of. This heart space is so much more in its realizing of who it is and of what it is to offer.

It is to be the clearest channel of love that is to be received by you for you.

It is in the clearing of this channel in which our love is always to flow through to you. Here you will begin to allow for the realization of this heart space to have the ability to let all flow in its ease of doing so with no hesitation or thoughts to be attached.

It is also to be allowed to feel empty within its inner realms.

In the emptiness that is offered to you to feel will allow for such powerful feelings of no restraints to hold onto or within this heart space. Be allowing here in the completeness of which all that is to be felt, so that no feelings of attachment are to be felt to remain. For it is in this understanding of this love that is ours to give to you, to receive, that you will feel the completeness of nothingness that is to be yours.

In this ever giving love there is to be nothing that is to grab hold onto you. In your ability to realize in this love you will feel the never ending ability of this love to always flow through to rejuvenate this of which it is that you are deep into the innerness that you are to be found.

To allow oneself to feel the confines of this space within, in regards to the loves or losses of another that are to gravitate within your surroundings of who it is that you are to be.

One will find that it disrupts and adds such discord to the innerness that is you to be realized.

For in the physical sense of love that you choose to see yourselves in relationships with another, it is felt like a restriction of such that holds us to them.

This is to be felt as a great experience upon the earthly boundaries that are to be this life that you are to reside within.

If it is to be seen as a chore or an effort to feel this love for another than it becomes a very weary process upon the physical body that is to hold this space for you.

Allow for the truth within you to be felt, to be spoken.

If you listen intently to this that the heart does speak, it is to be said that she is wise beyond your earthly years. She is in the greatest of understanding of all that it is that you so desired to be upon your becoming into this that you are to feel as your physical housing of this that you are to be.

In the acknowledgement of this greater love or as a reference to previous chapter your Big Love that is to be found.

It starts as small feelings of being very hard to connect to, in some cases the distrust within ones physical self has been allowed to wither and strangle this love so tightly that it is impossible or so you think to feel of this love to flow.

In witnessing this that you are to be, the stirrings which lay so deeply within you will feel as a slight upset within oneself to challenge the governor of this that be your physical body of which we suggest to be your mind. In this logical way in which it is to process the feelings of love that is to be ones such as yourself will feel this to falter within you as thoughts of distrust.

We are so often witness to these human emotions of love on the earthly planes that you are confined to witness, to feel, as though this is the true love and of how it should be interpreted by those that are on the receiving and giving ends of this love. This we offer is the human concept of love, which it is a pleasure at times to sit within you to receive.

In truth it is to be felt on a much grander scale this love that we speak of, for into the heart space it is to flow easily, effortlessly and unforgivingly to the creator of which is you in actual fact to your understanding of all that you are.

This love is timeless, forgiving and endless in its ability to receive of all that you are and to be ever offering to you as you stand strong within us realizing all that you are to be connected within.

Search deeply of this love for it is never not to be found.

It has a directness about it once found to realize that is to be heard so indiscriminately for you to feel. It is in searching for this love that the many of you are to get lost so to speak. We are present to see that it is to be felt as a mammoth effort that one must go through entirely. One is to allow themselves to feel loved not only of another's opinion but more importantly of their own response to themselves within these confounds of love.

This love that is yours to un-layer is you. This is the love that you must entice from within yourself with the remembering of all that it was to be. For this love is the greatest holder of you and the creator to share of this heart space together for the eternity that is to be yours to cherish within once again.

We challenge the many of you that think of this love as impossible to find, for in the way it is to be spoken about to the non-receiver seems unimaginable to the common senses of understanding. Many of those that re-discover this love are unwilling within to accept this love in its newness once more and are quick to dispel that it should not be felt at this intensity.

As receivers of the many of you already sitting into this love again we hear you share with us the feelings that this connection into this BIG LOVE has encouraged from within you.

This we offer to you to know and feel this love that is spoken often with gentleness and in great passion from those of you that have undertaken and chosen to allow for this unfolding to be discovered and are accepting of this big love within you.

We have been witness to you, as you have sat many times in readiness, understanding, quietness and love of yourself to be steady to allow for this love to be realized, as a different kind of love that is to be seen as the physical love. For it is far greater in retrospection of this love. This love that is the love of the all that is to be felt within your heart space often is to bring you to your knees in humbleness, it fills your spirit with tears of joy, allows for you to shout of this love from the rooftops so to speak. It governs within you this righteousness that is to be felt so strongly of correctness to be within you and it lights up your heart space flowing into all aspects of your life. It surrounds others that are to witness this unfolding of this big love that is to glow from within you to the extremes of all that we are to witness in the viewing of the heart space that you are to live within.

Be bold in your choosing of all that you are wishing to desire. It is in this space of love that is yours for you to witness these desires, dreams and wishes. All are sitting within this space of heart that is to be discovered, fear not an inner failure for it is not of so, to be received nor to be allowed.

It is not in failure that one does not succeed.

It is often in a sense of failure within the human ego or thoughts of it to be, that one feels as to be of not in receiving of such to be so. This we stand into you to correct of you this way to think of. It is in this that seems like not to receive or uncover so to speak that one is often to find the most revealing of thoughts to be found into this that they are to learn or know of.

It is in the un-denying of the true innerness that is you to be felt, to be heard that all that you are in asking of will not arrive.

So dream big in this heart space that is to be seen as the pureness of which it is that your truest desiring of you lays in. For she is to be found so receiving of you in this place that is waiting to be discovered.

Allow for her to be un-layered so that all the inner love that has sat within you until this time of unveiling can be remembered. So that you may feel the love that is to be the love that has created us and the worlds that are to be yours to enter into.

For there is to be no measurement or sizing put upon this feeling of love that is yours. It is to be seen in all of its greatness as the being of which it is that you are. And it is the being of which it is that we are of and in this that we sit as the one of source in all of creation that is to be seen as the all that we are.

We need never to second guess this feeling as it unveils within us being asked and allowed to rise. Know it rises in the exact time that you have requested it to be from the ethereal being of which you are to have entered from, into this understanding of this being of light that you are to hold steady within you.

This love is to be felt like your own personal signature of the true markings of this that you are. You will feel resonance with this love that is yours, for it is yours and yours alone to feel. It is not of another and no two big loves are to be found to sit within the same mold. For it is in this finding of this big love within your own heart space you are to witness your true unwrapping of the true speaker that is you.

Watch in great awe of this heart space as she delicately opens to this that is to be known as the greatest love of all.

In this opening are the sensations of all that is to be felt helping you to evolve into the being of light that you are to be seen as.

One is to stand in the strongest of graces of which it is that you are to allow for yourself to be held here. In the interpreting of this that you are for it is in your true state of this love to be seen, to be always felt that we are to find you in your asking of us to be within all that you are to be.

We ask nothing in return of this love to feel, for it is you that is the holder of this love. It is you that is the opener of this heart space that is to be yours to realize. So if it is to only offer yourself to us in your complete asking of to be recognized as the true you that you are to be. It is within and of this asking it is to be felt by you, this sense of recognition and trust of this love to surround you so that you will always know of your standing within all that is to be known as the creator of all that is.

"Willingly it is to us that you succumb. For it is in this wanting so deeply within that you are to hear of. That you will find the drawing of us to you so desirable of this that it is to be felt that no human or object will ever be in a position of which it is to hear from or offer to allow oneself to derail from your knowing passage into this ALL that you are becoming into"

[Message received in love of all that they be to know of]

CHAPTER SIX

LOSS IS YOURS TO FEEL

The longing of one internally is to always be allowing of loss to be felt. To think of wanting as to have, is to represent an attitude towards that of which it is that you do not have.

This is a loss as such to be thought of within yourself to feel.

It is in this feeling of loss that one is to strive and search ferociously into this that they do not know of what it is that they are searching of to become or to be.

Loss is to be seen as an attitude of what it is that one does not appear to have.

This is the only representation of loss that we appear to witness, in our observation of you that you are to experience. In the sense of not having or lack of, this is to stir many emotions within the human aspect of oneself including loneliness, grief, sadness, disappointment, regret and failure towards this feeling of loss to be yours to witness.

To feel the loss of another that is to be considered a part of you is very traumatic as it appears to be witnessed by us as your greatest fear upon this planet.

This we only have great love to offer to you to realize that this is to be viewed internally as the true aspect of oneself being realized into the truest being of which it was of them to become. We do not falter here to offer to you this to feel, to understand, to know of this being that has grown in attachment to oneself such as you is to be realized that all attachments as they appear are not of yours.

It was in their own deciding into this journey of which it was embarked upon that they were to decide of who it was that they were in this place of receiving to receive.

So you see, it is you that was the chosen one by them so that they could fulfil their integrity of this life that took them from you in this exact moment of complete understanding of all that they were to undertake, to receive, to gather knowledge into their own understanding of this that they are to become into this life time of existence.

See it as the ability of one to grow within, to expand, and to flourish into this being that they are in the desiring of to become. They are ever evolving into this that always is to grow, ever loving into their own understanding of the light being of which it is that they are to be a greater part of than it was to appear to be upon this planet with those that love grew into such love that is only from another to be given.

It is only in ones realization of this love that is greatest within that is to support them to grow into the becoming of which it is that they desired to become.

That all questions are to be resolved into the answering upon their reincarnation of this that they truly are to be received into once again as they are to sit within us the greatest love of ALL that is to be the complete source of Love.

In the human understanding of loss to be felt it is that the human form is to open up in such a rawness of regret towards what it is that they have not finished to be asked of them to provide. It is this that we regret to often to witness in your understanding of death. It is not of you to experience this that you feel you did not complete. For it is in their own asking of this passing in this time to receive that they were in the knowing of all that they were not to be to receive.

In one's death is the ability to remove all altercations into which it is that one appears to carry within them throughout this journey as such upon this planet.

Many are to find the instant release of these attachments in the form of emotions held so deeply within and physical ailments that are to be seen as the greatest of improvements towards explicit growth into which it is that one was choosing into their being of consciousness to be established for great growth within.

In sensing the great, aching loss of another that is to be felt as ever present within this life that is yours to feel as though it must be shared into a family or personal relationship in this now that you are to witness to be.

One must allow in their true heart of understanding that grief is YES a human form of love that was great to receive, to be felt and this is to know to be heard that it is to allow for this form, this loved form to be allowed to continue into their own space of receiving of which it is to be known as their transgressing into this ever evolving being of light that they are to always be realized into this that they are.

For they will not falter into their thinking of their passing rather as to seeing it as in the clearest of opportunities to revise, revisit and analyze all of this great life that they have lived this time, space, reality that was theirs to be involved into. They are to witness the deceasing of themselves in this the physical form so to speak, as a great opportunity of growth within them that is imminent to be upon their return.

They are always in such a fine place to witness, to hear, and to be with in spirit form to you those that are still in this place of not allowing of them to flow freely into this that they are to be.

In wanting of this to be, they ask of you and those that are cherished into this great love that is us, to be able to witness the offering within yourself to understand. It is to know of this love that it is far greater to all that think that they know great love in this life upon earth to be.

That it is not of any standard of which it appears to be here. For in this great love that is ours to offer in our entirety, they stand amongst the greatest of all that they are to be felt. To remember this love for them that they had simply forgotten into.

Sit within the love of the passed to allow for them to begin their new undertaking of which it is to be chosen by them.

So that you may feel their intentional love to you always for they have grown into another as such here so that they will always be in this place of offering to you, to hear of them as they whisper to you this that you are needing of to know.

They are ever present in regards to your asking of them to be. They are always in this place of recognition within, of which it is your heart space that they will forever be yours to cherish.

They do not or will not interfere into this life that you are still ever present in the role of which it is that you have chosen for yourself to be.

Allow for this physical love that will always be yours to carry in this life. Let it feel easy to carry and upon your return into your successful completion of all that you are to be realized into the becoming of yourself in your time of passing to be witnessed.

This cycle of death as one would call it here, is to be viewed as an ever present circle of determination within oneself. Its role is to allow for the continual growth and expansion into the ever growing ability that one is to realize within oneself to experience in the continuation of this soul that is the greater being of which it is that you are to realize within you in this life.

This being her search is for the ultimate attainment of source to be ever present within. To become at one again with this master that is to be seen as you, as me, and as all that is to be the truest calling card here to the true journeys of the souls and hearts of many that are being undertaken right alongside of you as you read into this understanding of death as you think of it in this human form that you are.

Expand your horizons of viewing death from one that is thought of as an ending. It is not to be seen in this sense to understand, for it is the greatest journey of oneself that is to be received and experienced. It is to allow for the complete growth of one to obtain all of which it is that they came here to experience. So that they may carry within them these experiences so that the next journey will be in contrast and be another offering to them to experience in the difference to this one that they so choose to be of this that you are to remember them as.

Death passes in a flurry of this that you are to understand as to view life in this existence of the human form of containment that you are.

It is to be seen in a completely different form of understanding from our viewpoint of which it is to understand. It is in your death or passing of this life that is to be of great rejoicing upon it to be for it is then that you are to return to us in this knowing of all that you have undertaken to be.

It is to be allowed for you to experience this complete cycle of life upon your planet to witness, to feel this feeling of loss as such for it is in your passing through of this that is to be revealed to you into your day of removal into this that we are.

You are to witness the strongest of urges to know of us once again and to always be ever present within us to this day of reckoning that appears as a great loss in the human form.

But it is not of a loss, but one of the greatest gains.

Again to be all that you are to be here within us once more.

Death is to surround you all at any moment of this inhabitation of oneself upon this planet. Whether it be in the human form or of an insect or animal that is to be a part of all that is to be felt. For many are transitioning in any given moment of their so choosing of this to be so.

It is a natural undertaking of the greater being that is to reside within such as you see yourself to be.

It is in this asking of to be that it is undertaken as the completeness into this journey to be seen as asked of.

Allow yourself to rejoice in this love of another that has been asked to be in happiness. To complete all that they were to undertake, to experience upon this planet to be theirs to have eternally into their being to grow and resolve of all that they set out to complete.

In your cherished moments these are ever capsulated into this time of your now to hold deep within you.

This you must respect within yourself as this that you are to become.

For there is never to be a finalization of all that is to be.

It is ever continual into this growth of knowing of to be.

We are to offer our ever gratefulness to you to be the light being that you are to become once more into us to be.

> *"We sit deeply within you all upon your asking of us to be allowed to be felt, to be heard.*
>
> *We honor all of which it is that you are asking of this to be.*
>
> *It is in you that we are of our greatest knowing of this love that is ours to offer to you to receive upon your truest asking of it to be felt."*

CHAPTER SEVEN

THE BABUSHKA DOLL SYNDROME

You dreamed and desired to be cherished and nourished by your innerness of this to never forget of the trueness that is to reside within you...

SO WHAT HAPPENED?

It appears you have been in the allowing of what it is known to me as The Babushka Doll Syndrome. It is in the innate ability that one has offered to oneself in the format to hide within each outer layer that has been laid upon your soul. This soul of yours that once was to shine so brightly that the thought of it being hidden from view was unimaginable to you.

To dispel thoughts of another's understanding of this that you are, is like applying another layer to your truest self of knowing so that it appears ever so indifferently to those who are in seeking to see themselves in the eyes of another.

This is where the transformation of the not so good starts to take place.

The more often that these layers are allowed to be offered to oneself throughout every moment of the Now that is to be undertaken within this life that you are to model yourself into this being of not of what it is that you are to be.

It is no wonder that ones such as yourself are to get lost within yourself, lost within your thinking of this that you are to be to find, for it becomes heavy this layering effect that is to take place ever so unnoticeably very often.

These gentle changes happen often without the noticing from the humanoid that you are to feel, to be. It is in the constant change of this that you are listening to, that these changes feel necessary. And if we are to be honest here for you to hear it is in the physical form of this life that you have undertaken that so many of these changes are accepted upon your form to carry, to hide behind that it feels necessary to do of this.

Life for you in this form begins with an eagerness, a refreshing want of this innate ability to learn, to flourish within this excitement that the baby that you are is to begin.

For it is in this eagerness to know that the steady remains of all that you are to be within is not yet forgotten of, so this fulfils you and your innerness to the knowing of all that you are to hold within.

You as the holder of all that you are is to start to feel this one that is to be your shining star within as it begins to take on the responsibilities of life as a human form.

Beginning with the role of a child being parented, within these ideals and expectations put upon by others. Next the form becomes a teenager that fights with her and her knowing of this life that she is thrust into the becoming of the woman that stares her down so hard at times that she is almost scared to step into this role of woman hood. The becoming of this woman that now contends with self-love and justification of all that she is to stand for, looks, appearances, associates, friends, lovers, careers and motherhood the list is endless it appears from our understanding of life upon Earth as we know of it.

This woman begins to journey most often into the maternal craving of to produce and nurture of ones to love all of her own. Into this feeds indirection within to the understanding of the mother that she is to become or in cases not to be so it becomes a constant shouting and negotiating within oneself, as to why she should or should not do of this that she has read, heard, felt or just assumed by thinking of this that appears to be done by others.

It is in this continual tug of war that it appears that this constant continual layer of another then another layer of this that I call the outer-ness of the Babushka doll syndrome. Here it is to start to feel heavy against the beautiful, ever-loving, ever knowing being of love that you entered here within the understanding of that you would always be true to.

In a quite instant, suddenly it feels to you as she is becoming ever so slowly lost to you, becoming a stranger in the distance that you once knew so well.

The contention that one is to now struggle within as the body's form naturally is to take shape to the treatment of neglect, stress that is contained within to never ask for help, lack of sleep, worrying, despair, grief, careers, not being enough, lacking within, of which it is to appear to be a serious job amongst those of you upon this planet.

Then it is of us to witness that you also add into the midst lovers, hardships, fights, strains within relationships with family members, partners and least we forget the children.

So it appears that this human form in all of her doing in trying to be the best version of herself to be. She has turned completely around to face ever so far away from the shining beacon of light that she is totally meant to be.

This view becomes very limiting upon the soul that is now searching for its true path to be asked of it again to be heard.

For she feels you still this you are to know, all of it is underneath all that has been laid upon her with each attachment to be felt to be recognized so indifferently as being her.

This is to feel like a continual misleading within her so that here is the start of the question that is to be allowed to rise and oh rise it will.

This innerness that is you, she will not be led astray.

It is in her connection to us and this perfect being of which it is that you are to be re-introduced to of all that you are to be realized into.

She will fight this syndrome that is to layer onto you so deeply at times that you are to become resistant to change, to movement in any which direction, in the ability to see oneself at all.

She will grasp at all that she knows within her love for you, this inner strength that she agreed to offer to you again, and again in you asking of this, is you. It is in your ability to shed, to release one layer off at a time, slowly it appears and often it will lead you to the rediscovering, the uncovering of, the unfolding of this that you thought of yourself as being, for these depths of layers that you feel are not you.

This is society and other people's offerings and your own worst opinions of your self being allowed to be heard to be placed upon you.

Stand strong when this asking is to be realized to hear, for it is in this asking that you will soon have an acknowledgement of the many outer doll shells that have layered within and upon you, to the deepest of hidings to the real you that is to be found once more if you are to allow yourself to start the search. To start the delayering process, to start to embrace this love that you have always been able to carry within, she must shine.

It is her one true job to connect you with us, to connect us with you always in her wanting and ours and to allow for you to be all that you are to be.

The babushka effect is like a ripple within a pond, if to be applied to this imagery. It is to start as a tiny splash that is to be contained within the center of the pond. It then becomes larger and larger to offer rings around oneself so as to not know of the previous ring that was once it to be.

So in this scenario of the ripple effect it is to gain momentum that is to fill the pond until it cannot sustain itself any longer. It then only has one choice, of which is to finally pitter out so (In human terms it becomes destructive within oneself until there is no choice as to hit rock bottom to find the strength within to climb upward) that it must return to the trueness that it was once to be in the beginning before anything was allowed to enter the water. This calmness, this serenity, this peace to be seen, to be felt is you that you were once to cherish to know of. For this is to be your pond and it is to be allowed for you to feel this original starting position before a pebble was thrown or such of a comment or object of emotion.

These are all layers of the babushka doll effect that we as humans living upon this planet have regrettably, upon the discovering of how lost we have become within trying to find ourselves.

So it is to offer here to you all to hear that in this your now is the perfect place to start, for there are to be no beginnings only steps along the way that work towards the true emerging of the you that you all have appeared to have forgotten.

You all have hidden away under all those layers of comments & opinions of others and inward directed conversations, dislikes and distrust of oneself.

It is time to turn towards that first layer, take a look and whether you like of what it is that you are looking at, trust that the voice that calls you, knows of you and all that is in her greatness. This is you and she is ever willing to help, to remodel, to re-align you back into the perfect being that you were to begin here into this now that you are.

Feel into this removal of the layers upon which it is that you allowed to be placed. Each one carries with it many emotions and thoughts of you that you think that you are, this you are to hear to know of, these you are not. Your true resonance is hidden deeply but not so deeply within as to never hear or feel her again.

For she is holding out her hand to be held by yours.

Our offering to you, is this that you shall know of, you are to begin to encounter, that this is your own personal babushka doll that you are to find. So let your journey begin to unfold one disheartening, displeasing, grotty layer at a time.

It is unforgiving work it feels, with in this that you are to experience. Stand strong fast as you watch to witness, as you begin to see the light that is you that has no choice but to respond to the layers that are being removed. For you will be blinded by all that you see within yourself to be once more.

It is to be known in Russia the true meaning of the so named babushka doll aka[Matryoshka Doll] is to be one known literally as meaning little matron.

The Latin root word of Matryoshka is mater, which means mother, motherhood, family and fertility all influences the meaning of these Russian nesting dolls. Being thought to have originated into existence for the Russian culture to have what is to be considered having a close knit family. And is common and important with many generations and extended family playing an important role within the family model.

In my offering to be received, to feel, to translate my thoughts are of the dolls to be representative of layers placed upon oneself ,in which it is to see oneself as the hidden baby babushka character within.

So this is to be asked of oneself to always think of themselves as the mothering or childlike aspect of oneself never to be forgotten, one of nurture and love to be held within themselves.

To always be allowing for the continual support of others in kind and of generous nature to be witnessed by you and to be offered generously by you in return, and to see that the surrounding of oneself with outer support built of trust, is to be felt deeply within all that you are to know of your true self that's to be always the love of all that you are within.

CHAPTER EIGHT

INNER SANCTUARY

Step into my inner garden,
Sit still for a while,
Feel the peace and serenity,
As it fills my wholeness from within,
Contentment washes over me,
Complete into this that I am
In this place that I crave to sit
I realize now, this is my Inner Sanctuary.
I am not lost here although to some I appear so.
It is here I AM found into ALL, that I be.

The becoming of the asking to find your inner sanctuary, is where it is to be felt rising and stirring from deep within.

This is to be seen, to be felt that this is the place that so many of you are craving to find to feel .These feelings of wanting to be, to find that inner peace that so many of you are to feel as a need, it is to want of this to be.

Know that this is you already, for if you are to sit in your quietness of all that you are, even for a moment in this space that is yours to create, you will endeavor to note without fear of doubt that this innerness that you are to search for will be heard, to be felt, to know, that this is the inner sanctuary that is yours to feel this wholeness within.

The inner sanctuary, your inner sanctuary is to be felt as this reservoir of love that is placid in its calmness to witness.

For it is spoken of as to be seen as a scared temple, that many attempt to hide the truth in which it is to be held secretly by those that have found it to be within. It is to be known that the true inner sanctuary that is for all of you to witness, to feel, as your own. It is part of the whole complete sanctuary that is to be allowed to sit within you, allowing for you to feel this magnificence that is all that you are to be experiencing within. For it is to be ever offered to you and all that search to find.

For it is of us that you will soon realize that this is to be your innerness of which it is to be called your inner sanctuary.

In the knowing of all that love is to you, to be felt, to be in the ability to receive and to know of your worthiness to receive all that is to be offered.

There are no limitations placed here upon this offering.

So it is in this that you call the inner sanctuary that you think to be unattainable by you, or as not able to be found by the many that are searching.

We ask of you; give up this fruitless search constricted by denial that sits within you of being unworthy of this that stops you from seeing to feel that this inner sanctuary comes with only the attachments of peace, faith, trust into all that you are to listen to, to resonate within for this is you.

This is your inner sanctuary just becoming into a different name, this name of trust within yourself so to speak of, for this inner sanctuary will always be found within you and in your asking of it to be realized into.

This inner sanctuary is allowing in its righteousness of being all that it is to be to offer to you. It opens to offer with no limitations of this that you must be, for if you are to sit within your openness of all that is to be honest within you.

You will find the deeper it will be that you are allowed to sit within, for the inner sanctuary is you in your trueness of the true you that you are in this that you are, in this that is to be your now to recognize.

For there is to be no other time that is to be more relevant to you in this form that you are to be, but of only this your Now. In this that you are.

It is here you are to sit in your truth to be heard of this that guides you, directs you, and loves you intentionally of all that you are to ask.

It is to be seen as your higher ever present self that resides here in this that you ask to be your inner sanctuary.

Witness as you open the inner heart space of this that holds your inner sanctuary at its utmost present position of which it is to be felt.

It is to be said that in this inner sanctuary much of you that sits is to be bathed in this love that is ever filling, ever caressing, ever continual for you to feel, that in this inner space that you have recognized as it is within you is to be always in wanting to be filled with this love that is generated by the creator of all that sits within this space.

So that it may be felt lovingly when it is to overflow into all that you feel yourself to be, touching, caressing, intertwining into this form that you have chosen on the outside to be.

This love is non directional in its path of offering and it is to find its own way of offering to the outward worldly presence that you sit within to be recognized as you this that you see in your earthly eyes to be.

This love glows brightly and ever finding to all that sit alongside of you to feel of this love is the true meaning of to find your inner sanctuary. For in this place of peace, calm and faith of love that is to be yours is for all that surround you to be able to sit within so they too may realize of this magnificent garden. This blossoming space that is to grow within them upon their realizing of this, to ask of this love that is to be the love of all that has stood to be recognized into their becoming of.

We delve deep into the understanding of all that you are to be willing to see yourself as you are, as you stand here in this place of to receive for in your asking of this to find, this magnificent place of love it is that you realize that the search ever so continual is of utmost importance to you. For your search has been this that you are to become. It is only in this placement of you that you are now to read of these pages that maybe the slightest urges of asking are stirring within you, or like many that have come before you are feeling lost in the surging within that this opening is offering to them to find to feel.

Realize in this that all inner sanctuary's, yours included are of a vastness of the largest ocean, universes or the knowing of all that you could possibly imagine. For these inner sanctuary's that are to be asked of, are to resonate into this that we are to all be a part of. Sitting together in this receiving of all that is to be known as the one trueness that is to hold us deeply within its own inner sanctuary that it found open in its creation of, into this being of which it is to ever continually evolve into being.

This inner sanctuary is to become to you the prevalent understanding of all that you are asking to stand into. Let it be in this space of recognition that this honest knowing within you that is correct in every form of its existence to be recognized by you as you. It is in this space to speak of one is to sit, to feel into their own understanding of this that is your inner sanctuary and all that is to be filled with that of which is to be offered to those that surround you. In you're asking of to find this inner sanctuary you will be rewarded with the knowing of that this is not of yours to hide into or hide its revealing of. For this is to be the inner sanctuary that one is to share, from the words of many that have been truly guided to speak of and to hear of that out of this that is yours becomes this for many to become. So in this it is to offer up your inner sanctuary for many to choose to sit within for the more that are to become knowing of this holiness that is to be offered to the worlds, the more we are to grow into our expansion of becoming this magnificent light filled with beams of love for all to stand within in their own perfection of this that they are to be realized into.

> *Connecting into your inner sanctuary we are to offer this as guidance to be received by you to feel a satisfaction into the efforts of all that you are to contemplate as to begin.... If one is to connect into their own inner sanctuary one is to know that the beginning of such has already begun.*

For it is within you that the eternal light of all that you are to be realized out of is already in the firm belief of this knowing. Allow for the gentleness within time to be received and in this asking of it to be felt one must be resilient to all that they will feel upon their journey to ask, to feel this that is to be revealed within them. For it is not a place as such to view into for it is ever surrounding you, ever flowing within you, ever completing you and ever recognizing all of that it is that you are to live within.

For there is to be no greater asking other than to ask for all that you are to become into. To be heard, to receive so that you may feel compassion as you sit into your inner sanctuary knowing of this that appears to be thought of as yours is not and in the offering of this to all that are in the asking of to witness to see within. That this is the truest, most grandest place that you will find your inner sanctuary to be, so that it can be realized by you as the most ever present place in which you desire to sit.

My wanting for you is to feel as my inner sanctuary becomes of one with yours.

No matter the stage of which it is, whether this be still to be discovered or to be fully realized as the complete inner sanctuary that it is every growing, ever evolving, ever asking of. For in this that I stand my garden, my inner peace, my inner calm, my inner love that is all that I am to be, is that I may find you. So that we may stand in our own inner sanctuaries as they touch effortlessly into the becoming of simply the one that shines of light, love and all that is to be fulfilled into the allowing of to be reunited always into this that we are to become together once more.

CHAPTER NINE

WISDOM WITHIN

Let flow of all that is to be your inner wisdom.

For in the asking of this to be felt, to be received, to be heard, in this you will not falter as to the truest being of which it is that you are to be.

Brace yourself deeply in coherent understanding of all that you ask of loudly and confidently in the graciousness that is yours to be.

Know that it has been heard to be offered.

It is in your own understanding of this that it is to be your written wisdom for you to receive, to know of which you will find the soul of which it is in your asking of, was of you to ask.

This inner wisdom that we speak so fondly of is of course us and the all that is to be the ruler in all that you are to place your faith into.

For if it is not of an understanding between you and of us than it is not to be felt truly deeply within your own true heart space. And it is in this space of heart that it is to be felt the strongest of knowing into this that you are to confide into with.

Our wisdom is ancient in its knowing of this that you are to be, so allow for all that we are to offer upon your asking of to be gifted to you to feel, to be guided into this place that you are to now stand.

For this is your wisdom of the innerness that has been carried deeply within you many times over of your asking of to receive to know of all that you must feel that is to be contained within this soul that is yours. It is of this asking heard within that one is to cherish, to honor of her journeys' that she has to feel as though they are in her becoming of to be.

She resists the urge to manipulate of all that you do, for in this she must not, but to sit quietly in knowing of this that she is to be. You will allow her to trace out the pathway of your existence into this that be a map so that you can follow, for it is the map of your inner wisdom that is to speak to you fondly of all that you desire, dream and crave, for it is in this wisdom that you are to feel of her.

Inner wisdom is allowed to sit dormant for eternity if need be and if not asked of to hear. For it is in your asking of that this be written into you to receive. It is with much expectation of this that you are to feel this need to want to know the answers that are burning upon your soul, so that it cannot resist the urge any longer and the need to rise on up within, are of the truest intentions of all that will be hers to offer.

It will appear as in disbelief of what it is that you witness to hear, for it starts small this we know as such of not to want to be willing to be allowed to think of us in this way.

Let your innerness of which it is to know of, the wisdom that is to be great and foreboding within you to surface. For she feels knowing no other pathway of which to allow for herself to connect continually eternally to the true offerors of all that source is to be.

She is a benevolent being of love that has scriptures written wholly and soulfully upon all that she is. These are your inner wisdom messages of trust, truth and faith and power into this that we are of which it is that you are seeking.

You hold within you this power of great that is if only it is to be seen, to be felt for and of you. And it is to be heard so deeply within so that it will soon disrupt all of which you think that it is to be true within and surrounding of you.

For this written wisdom that is felt eternally into your knowing of this that you are. Stand tall into the meeting of this you are to become. You will interpret all of this as your truth to speak of and this is your platform to stand alongside all of us that are to know of this wisdom that is to be felt as the finalization into this becoming of this that you are to crave to be.

Stand into us with your open hearts of love to be filled so intently with this love so that you will feel to hear of the greatest wisdom that is to ever have been written and this you will feel as yours and ours to share of.

For it is in this knowing of that it will be heard again and again, over and over always from within you as you are to feel to speak of this that is your own true soul offering of us to you.

Your written wisdom is deemed to be the all that you are to be in your place of which it will be revealed to you into this that you are to realize yourself of this that we are.

It has been written in many different languages, scriptures, etchings and symbols and times of old to understand and to stand into, of this we know.

For it is of us in your asking of which it was to offer this to you in many times of to ask that you did to receive.

In all that is written within you is much of what it is that you are to have experienced and are to be in the ever present ability of which it is to know of as your NOW.

For it is sitting deeply into you these words and writings of the realness that is you to be felt.   These words are your writings and stories of the many lives that are yours of this that you be and it is understood into the finest of details of all that you have written upon oneself to be of, to be asked to discover, to experience into.

Allow for these ancient carvings of such to be known to be yours and of you in all that they hold the writings of truth that they be. For it is to be your secret language of this that you are to understand to be the biggest part of to be.

In your truth it is to know of that all that you write upon oneself and in every newness that is written to be held, to be of a witness for you to remember into your times as such that you will transverse into this that you have wrote with us once more.

It will be of the greatest discovering of this that you became here into this life of the now that you are to hold so deeply into.

For this is your time to write once more upon your soul so to speak. So that you are to always remember of this greatness that you so desired to add into your collectiveness of being that you are a part of.

We ask of you NOT to write of intentions, for this leads to foreboding within the soul that you be. For out of intention comes loss, regret, sadness, grief into what was not to be of the physical to notice. It is in your deepest knowing of this that we be that you will feel to write of ALL that you shall become. For it is of this true speaker that holds your wisdom lovingly that allows for ALL that is intended to be of, will be shown to you to see.

CHAPTER TEN

THIS ONE IS FOR YOU

In this offering, I AM being guided to write of myself and my journey thus far. I was, if I am to tell you the truth very reluctant and hesitant to speak of my journey as it appears to me to offer.

You see my story is no more exciting or extravagant, neither more interesting, than that of yours. It is to be spoken of this life of mine, for it too has been edited with trials and tribulations of life yet in the same breath of which I AM to speak also filled immensely full to the brim of love, joy and moments of such desire to be as it would appear no more than any that I have heard to be presented to myself being told of by others and their own stories to tell.

This I have to explain that in my becoming of which I still am in the process of, for it is to never cease this becoming of the;

I AM THAT I DESIRE TO BE.

In my asking to hear the answer within myself to....

WHO IS IT THAT I AM.

I heard this tiny whisper, ever so quiet, it was gently nudging me from within this that I am to be in my NOW.

Well this whisper and gentle nudging soon gave way to a gnawing into myself that I could no longer ignore.

So I decided to listen, to follow, to ask, to allow, to doubt, to falter and even will myself to conquer all fears and doubts that I held within myself strongly and some of which I still do to this present day, ever working to progress into this that I truly desire of to be.

The truth is. In this process that I chose to commit to, to listen to, to recognize with, to practice sitting in my sacred space of love daily.

I found me, this journey of deep sourcing and unveiling, de-layering within the All, that I thought as a human I was to be.

This work within, the unfolding, the opening of my heart space to the 'callings' of the true being that I'm to be realized as this to become. For I am ever becoming this I know, but I was to hear of this I Am that I was to ASK of.

I discovered there is nowhere to hide within the spiritual path that one is to decide to undertake for this path is yours alone. It is long and at times appears never ending, challenging to the ego to acknowledge, for All that is revealed within you is asking of you to allow yourself to be heard, to receive, to be felt, to live and to be love.

You will discover this that is you, is that of which I AM.

In love I stand into ALL that is powerful within me.

To speak of this love has given me the true being of which it is that I now remember her being. In her it is this that I feel the confidence of her allowing me to speak lovingly of all that she is to be?

She will forever remain intentionally recognized within me for it is to be said I do not desire to forget this being that I am to be ever again. I will always allow for my light that is held so lovingly within to shine as bright as she can, in this light it is that I am to feel me, so that all that I stand alongside of in this life that I am to live as me, is to be always felt by another so that Love as we are to be full to brim within is to be able to overflow.

This love is to be felt no differently by all of those that are just becoming or fully committed into this that they are to be.

This is the I AM that I have asked and searched to find, for you see my questions were or are to be no different to the ones that you may be asking of yourself to hear in this now that is yours to offer.

So acknowledge this love within you that is the true voice to your words.

Allow for her to be bold in her asking for it is of you that she knows in the truth of which it is that you are to be.

Stand strong in your space, embrace all that is to unfold for you, relish in the discovering of the truest version of you, no matter how uncomfortable and disheartening it may get, and this I promise, you will never look backwards to glance of the old that once was, for in this unfolding is the truest you to flourish into this that you are of......

The 'I AM' that you are ALL forever within.

In the asking of which it is that I was wanting of to receive, it became this to be.

My request to find or to be presented rather with the discovery of a yellow feather, the bigger and brighter I asked it to be the more the meaning of it would surely prove to me in the asking of it to be. (This was to be my test of spirit, to prove to me that they were of all that they speak. I think all that evolve into this understanding of spirit to be within them to find will and have offered these little challenges to those that love us with such of intention to always be this that we are. This is of the human mind to think is it not?) It was after some time that I realized or thought that I was not to receive of what I was asking for, YES; it was in disappointment that I felt that I had been betrayed in a sense that my asking of was not to be heard by the divine or at best even worthy of to be heard.

This was to be myself sitting into the doubt of the human form that I can sit into at times and to negate all of this that I am that I know of myself to be.

I witnessed myself in such self-doubt of this to come to me that I gave up on all that I thought I knew of what it was that I loved of them so to speak… It was in my human feelings and emotions that I was to feel betrayal and distrust of this that they always speak of and that is "to ask is to be given", this I felt, I was to question the truth of this statement and what it meant to me.

So to clarify this a little more of which to understand of what it was that I was asking for this yellow feather to represent to me. It was that this yellow feather was to be my sign that I was on my journey to discover and to be realized into this that I was to be. I didn't think at the time of asking that this was too much to ask for to receive, little did I know that in my connection with the All that be and their answering of this that I asked was to be an answer that I was not prepared to receive.

These are the words I heard clearly and in a boldness in truth and love for me to receive.

It is not of us to give you this yellow feather that you ask of to be a sign that you are to be upon your path of your life's journey to begin. For in this Tanya you are to hear to know of that it is this life that you are into that you must realize is to be seen as your journey. There is to be no beginning of such as in this life to be for it is within us that you began and have been becoming in your whole entirety of this that you are to be of us. So to ask of this yellow feather to represent a beginning is not for you to receive. If we were to offer you a yellow feather as a request for you to receive to represent your beginning of, it will fall upon your death of this that you are in the human form so to be the complete receiving of which it will be that your journey into us of us has begun once more. To stand into this that we are into this knowing of all that you are to become of this eternal ever fulfilled being of love, light and grace to be.

So it is in this that we do not offer to you in your asking of this to be, for it is not of us to give what cannot be offered in truth and love and into the completeness of which it so shall be asked of it to be. You will one day be in the holding of to have this beautiful yellow feather but in this we offer to you. This is when you will feel the true meaning of this yellow feather. Know it will be felt without a doubt that it was yours to receive in this time, space, reality of your now that of it is to become the ALL that you are so worthy and knowingly of to become once more. It is into this that we be that you are to be, so much into this love that is us to be you. That into this becoming once more upon your returning you will be gifted with the truest remembering into the meaning and knowing of all that we are to offer for you to receive.

It is not to be forgotten that you intended of, but to be simply into your asking of to be able to be discovered of this that you be and to ask of it to open in your timing of which it was to ask that you will remember to know of this that you are in whole of to be.

So it is in this my now that I allow for all that is offered to me to feel, to see, to hear, to receive of that it is to be in the exact asking of such it was asked to be received by me.

In this my ever knowing, ever present essence of this love that is to reside in me of this beautiful being that I AM that I will always stand into you of this that you are as you are to stand into your absolute perfection of the ALL that you be.

It is in this practice of you that I am to sit into this place of which it is to receive clearly, intentionally and boldly directed by all that I am in the hearing of the all that you be.

> *Here I share my thoughts as I am to know of my practice.*

Feel as you are in the mind to allow, for it is not of thought that is needed here into this that you ask to sit. All is always not seen to be as it appears, for it is of this magnificence that we be that we see you in the light of this that you are. Feel as you allow for this light to wash across you ever so gently at first almost in a sense of non-recognition of this that feels misplaced upon first contact or connection. This is the love of us and you that we be entwined together always into that you will feel. We ask of you to release to offer to us all that you are to think of yourself to be and not to be, for here into us that you sit you are just as you should be.

No attachments to thought here is needed, as you will be guided into your daily practice with ease and confidence if you are allowing of the human mind to step away or into the back ground, if only just for a moment as complete inner peace is to wash over you to feel. It is in this knowing of awakening to the new beginning that you will feel of this to be felt that ones such as yourself will feel the urgency within to be more of this that you are to sit into. Allow the impatience of this to be felt gently and reluctantly each and every time and it will naturally find its own rhythm within you to be offered as complete in its difference of that to another to explain to speak of their experiences.

You are of us; so into this it is to offer here to you to feel, to hear, that all that you are is us in the offering only into your asking of which it is to be felt to receive by you. We stand ever so loving into you. In this place that you feel as breath, a nothingness that caresses you and calms you like no other place, or person that you have ever known. It is here that you begin to remember to know of the all that you are the biggest part of. Release all of which it is in this human form that you are, for there is to be no form of such that you think of yourself to be into here that we are to be recognized into. In here it is and to offer an 'in here' is ill relevant to speak of, for you must know of this to hear that you are always in us. It is to be offered, for you are of us, so it is of us that you be always in your allowing of all that you are to be the true realizer of this great love that you are. Watch with a fascination as your limitless is to appear and your desiring of this to find within yourself regularly is to become a wanting within itself and is to call to you ever so loudly and directly into your everyday thoughts of this life that you live, we have heard it to be spoken in comparison to 'such a greatness that you are to find within here once more and to feel such of a completeness that is you'. In your connection into us it is to be felt by you, ever knowing that you are this love and all that sit into you are to be seen only in this new found view of everlasting love. Many are to ask to search of the how to guide so to speak into which it is to be conducted or taught to others.

> *We offer here to you to know of this that you are, so you be and are already of.*

It is to be felt within you and in your way of which you feel is to be known as correct within you. Trust of us we say to be heard by the many that it is in your feeling of this that be seen as the ever loving place that it is described often as. That there is to be no mistake or wrong doing upon your sitting into. For you will not be mistaken of all that we be in you upon your realizing into this that you are. For it is in you that we are found as in us that you are of. Know of all that you are to be is the truest form of you and she will not serve you wrong as you are to feel it within you that you are.

Many offerings, directions and realizing's are offered to you with eternal opportunities to discover you in the purest essence of all that you be.

Many life's previously lived to learn are opened into your viewing of them to be a part of your understanding into this that you are.

Feel as your guides, loved ones past and present offer to you much in offering, support and love.

Strength and weaknesses become you here into this that you are to discover, embrace all that is offered for there is no darkness here that is not warranted as any offering to you. It is to be a self-discovering of oneself to know of to move forward into this journey of progression of you to become.

Feel as you unwrap the All of this that you are here, no guidelines or instructions are needed.

In this space of love one is to feel our commitment to you, as the one of your own knowing of such that we are. For here it is to flow freely, lovingly, ever knowingly, of ALL that is to be the beautiful you, within ME...

IN ONE WORD YOU SIMPLY ARE TO,

NOTES / INTENTIONS

Please use of these pages as you will. Allow for the knowing of ALL that you are to receive, to write, is in absolute of ALL that you are...

to be...
to hear...
to know...

....
....
....
....
....
....
....
....
....
....
....
....

NOTES / INTENTIONS

NOTES / INTENTIONS

www.ingramcontent.com/pod-product-compliance
Lightning Source LLC
Chambersburg PA
CBHW070309010526
44107CB00056B/2539